FOR
EDEN + AUTUMN

THE MOST IMPORTANT DAYS
OF YOUR YOUNG LIVES ARE
THE DAY YOU WERE BORN
(WHICH YOU HAVE ACCOMPLISHED
WITH GREAT FANFARE + SUCCESS)
AND THE DAY YOU BOTH
LEARN WHY!

THE WHY WILL COME AS YOU
EXPLORE THIS WORLD AROUND
YOU + THE WONDER YOU WILL
DISCOVER WITHIN YOU!

GOOD LUCK IN
YOUR JOURNEY'S

Mark Duffield
7/7/20

AS I RECALL . . . The Explorer

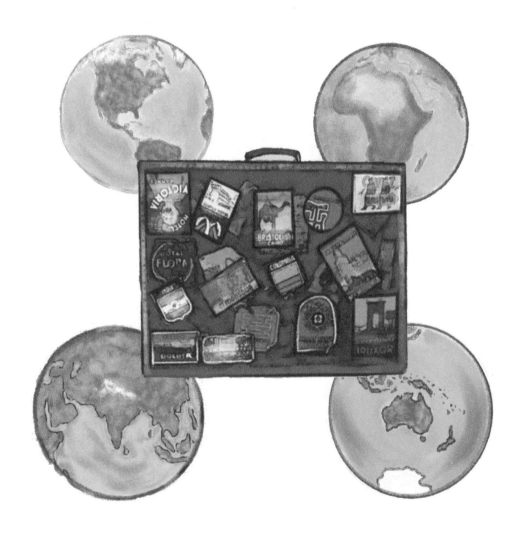

AS I RECALL . . . The Explorer

Mark Duffield

Illustrated by Nancy O'Hearn
Postscript by Sharon Duffield

Strategic Book Publishing
www.sbpra.net

For information about special discounts for bulk purchases, please contact Strategic Book Publishing, Special Sales, at bookorder@sbpra.net.

ISBN: 978-1-68235-850-4

Dedication and Special Thanks

Dedicated to:
Jim and Sue Duffield

Special Thanks to:
Sara Israel
Sharon Duffield
Upstairs Downstairs
Laura and Bob Cousineau

Preface

"There are three rules for writing a novel (story). Unfortunately, no one knows what they are."

W. Somerset Maugham

Rules? No idea. But...a story I have.

AS I RECALL: The Explorer is the third in a series of *AS I RECALL* stories. The series and the main title is an homage to our father who penned his autobiography a few years before he passed. He titled it *AS I RECALL*. It was a fascinating history of a life that started in the horse and buggy days and journeyed to the exciting days of space exploration, culminating with a man landing on the moon.

Our story here is a slight departure from the previous two stories. *AS I RECALL: Fireflies in the Night* and *AS I RECALL: Wings of Remembrance* were memories of actual events. In this story we have based it as before on actual events and true environments, but have recreated some events to enhance and highlight our true purpose: to showcase the loving character of our father, who demonstrated over a lifetime so many qualities and so many loving gestures, surprises, and supports that, above all, encouraged his children to explore the world.

Our story begins with the actual launching of our fabled boat, the *Explorer*. It's journey becomes a symbol of all the journeys we would actually take in our lives. The return of the *Explorer* is the idealized version of what is gained by leaving home, exploring the world and returning home once again to a welcoming safe and loving harbor that only family can provide. I think it is in our human nature to leave the security of our homes and, like Ulysses, search for adventure, with its many dangers and challenges, that nurtures our growth, sense of freedom and independence and ultimately makes our lives worth living. Some, like me, yearn for one more quest. I had many thrilling quests around the world. I traveled across much of Africa, sailed down the Amazon River in a small boat and had dozens of adrenaline-filled adventures on six continents. But like the fictional Ulysses, I had only one goal in mind...it was to find my way home. Our story here is the launching of such a life.

Throw off the bowlines

Sail away from safe harbor

Catch the trade winds in your sails

Explore—Dream—Discover

—Attributed to Mark Twain

OUR STORY BEGINS HERE:

AS I RECALL, on any given summer day my twin sister Sharon and I could be found skipping stones from the banks of the little pond at the end of our street. Dad taught us how. He always said that we alone cannot change the world, but, like skipping stones across the water, we can all leave a ripple. And the best way to leave a ripple was to explore the wonders of the greater world beyond our little pond. He was always preparing us for life's voyage and sharing what could be learned by traveling: love and respect and empathy for all cultures. The fellowship of the human family was all-important. He and my mother had traveled widely around the world, and travel was always encouraged.

These thoughts all came home one particular summer day: July 7, 1956. Sharon and I were celebrating our seventh birthday. Birthdays were a big deal in our tight-knit neighborhood. Readying for the big event, parents made sure their children passed a rigid inspection, their faces washed—behind the ears, too—hands cleaned, and hair combed. Then fussing over wiggling, squirming children, parents dressed their charges up in their Sunday best: little suits, bow ties, and Buster Browns for the boys and crinoline party dresses, hair ribbons, and Mary Janes for the girls. These were the early days of innocence on Lake Drive in Darien, Connecticut.

Into our tiny backyard they marched, carrying their little birthday gifts for Sharon and me. The gifts were placed on the large picnic table in the middle of our yard. Colorful balloons and crepe paper adorned the table. Our backyard was small. It was connected to every other backyard in the neighborhood, with easy and welcome passage through entrances on split rail fences. These were such trusting times.

Of course, we were partial to our backyard. My dad had made it into a wonderland of nature and beauty. Flowerbeds full of colorful snapdragons, tulips, marigolds, asters, and zinnias sprouted everywhere. A small vegetable garden surrounded a tomato patch, and birdhouses built by Dad hung everywhere. Vines of Concord grapes draped the split rail fences. Over its entrance, a trellis of pink roses bloomed. Another trellis of roses adorned the garage wall. Two apple trees and a Japanese maple rose above a rich green lawn of velvet straight out of an oil painting. A sandbox by the garage and a new swing set in the corner of the yard made our backyard a child's paradise of butterflies, lightning bugs, ladybugs and honeybees.

My mom disappeared into the nearby kitchen and returned with a birthday cake, and everyone sang "Happy Birthday" to us. Presents were unwrapped and outpoured: paper dolls, barrettes, squirt guns, Colorforms, Play-Doh, Matchbox cars, a Slinky and the game of Sorry and a lot of candy. After cake and ice cream and watermelon, the games began. Games of hide-and-seek, sardines, tag, and watermelon-seed-spitting contests were par for the course at all birthday parties back then. You never wanted it to end, but like all things . . . it did.

Suddenly the yard was empty and Mom was preparing dinner. We were seated at the picnic table once again. Paper place mats, paper plates, and plastic forks recycled from the birthday party and Mom's German potato salad and deviled eggs and Dad's barbecue chicken filled the table. After dinner we heard the ringing bells of the Good Humor Ice Cream Truck and ran out in front of the house for a double orange-and-grape popsicle.

Whew! What a day! And it was only seven o'clock! Nightfall was still two hours away. The summer evening light was wonderful, a warm golden glow. For young children, however, it also signaled time for bed. But on this day, there was more to come. My father got up from the table and walked over to the garage. When he returned to the picnic table, he carried in his hands the greatest of all birthday gifts for Sharon and me: a beautiful, magnificent pond boat! A model sailboat . . . a sloop!

Oh, my goodness! A large sloop! My dad handed us a captain's log so we (or my mother) could record the sloop's details and dimensions to make sure everything was shipshape. It was a fore-and-aft rig, almost in every aspect an exact copy of a real sloop. The workmanship was superb. The hull was twenty-eight inches of glossy fiberglass, white upon turquoise marked with a maroon Plimsoll line, thirty-two inches with the bowsprit. The deck had mahogany planks. Positioned on deck was a small cabin, only three inches high and seven inches long, ringed with four small windows on each side. There was a small companionway stern side that led to some imaginary luxury quarters below. Beam to beam at its widest point it was eight inches across. A sturdy captain's wheel, tiller, rudder, and keel were things of wondrous geometric symmetry. Running along the gunwales were brass cleats and various pulleys and lines. It was slick and handsome from stem to stern. But what took your breath away was the sail—the magnificent white sail attached to a three-foot mast billowing on its boom from the light backyard breezes. My goodness, I could barely breathe. Sharon and I were speechless. While Dad attached the jib sail, we circled the picnic table, investigating every minute detail. Sewn on the mainsail by my mother was a large red number seven.

On the hull, on the port side, Dad had painted Sharon's name. On the starboard side he had painted the name Mark. At the stern below the transom he had painted, in gold, *THE EXPLORER*. WOW! For sailing purposes, Dad put an eye screw at the stern. From this he attached a fishing line, yards and yards of it attached to a spool. Dad told us the word sloop was related to the Old English slupan, meaning "to glide."

"So," he said, "shall we take the ship for a glide tomorrow?"

Early the next morning, with boat in hand, we walked to the small pond at the end of our street. We set up near Turtle Rock, a boulder near the shore where painted turtles loved to sunbathe and swim among the lily pads. Dad placed the *Explorer* in the water and gave it a gentle shove.

He handed us the line, and Sharon and I took turns feeding it out from the spool. Well, there was not much breeze that day and the *Explorer* didn't sail far. It seemed reluctant to move. It sat becalmed and still . . . so we reeled the *Explorer* back in and went home.

***

A week later, Dad drove us to Pear Tree Point Beach on Long Island Sound, only a couple of miles from our house.

We arrived very early in the morning before beachgoers filled the sandy shore. It was here we would launch the *Explorer* on her maiden voyage and really put her to the test. No problem with wind here: there was plenty of it, blowing straight out towards Long Island across fifty miles of open water. Dad thought the water was calm enough to launch.

The three of us waded knee deep into the water. Dad placed the boat in the water, adjusted the sails, and handed us the spool of line.

"Let it out gently. Allow the wind to fill the sails. A little bit of line at a time," he said. The waves were mere ripples and the *Explorer* handled them with ease. Sharon and I took turns letting out the fishing line. What fun it was to watch our sloop sail forth toward the swimming floats, past them, and out into the sound and open blue water.

Meanwhile, the concession stand was opening and Dad left us to buy some breakfast for his two captains.

YUP! Left us in charge! Well, before you know it, the wind had picked up. The Explorer had become a mere speck on the horizon. Yards and yards of fishing line had run its course. Before we knew it, all we held was an empty spool.

When Dad returned, the *Explorer* had completely vanished from view. Poor Dad!

The boat was too far out to see, find, or rescue, and there were too many twin tears to dry in one day. No words of comfort or solace could bring our treasure back.

Except for muffled sobs and sniffles, the ride home was completely silent. That night, dinner was like attending a funeral. Before sitting down at the table, Dad scoured the night sky . . . for words, I guess. Finally he spoke up. We felt sure the admonishing lecture about responsibility was about to commence. Instead, he began by noticing the full moon of days before. It had now become a "gibbous moon," a little more than half full. But he knew it would become full again in the weeks to come.

"Like the phases of the moon, we change and become full once again. Everything returns home in its own good time. All circles eventually complete themselves," he said. He then offered this bit of wisdom from John A. Shedd: "A ship in harbor is safe, but that is not what ships are built for."

"Ships are built to explore," he told us. "Just because we can no longer see our ship, doesn't mean it's not there. It's out there over that part of the horizon not yet visible to us today. But someday. Right now, let's take pleasure in and imagine the grand voyage the *Explorer* is experiencing now. So many exotic ports of call all over the world to visit and so many cultures to greet and meet and learn from. Think of it—Europe, Asia, India, Africa, and South America, all cheering wildly when the *Explorer* glides in! Its billowing sail full of love, fraternity, and friendship, emblazoned with the number seven waving its greeting to all."

Several things changed that night for both Sharon and me. We could, like Dad said, clearly imagine all the wonderful adventures our little sloop was experiencing . . . and that night he planted a seed in us to discover the explorer within, and follow the journey of our little sloop over the watery parts of the world.

***

Life goes on, of course, and memories both sad and pleasant flicker and dim while being replaced by new ones. We grew up. Dad provided so many wonderful and thoughtful chapters in our life. That one great memory melded into another and our little sloop once again became a mere speck on the horizon among all the other specks. All these little brush strokes, however, became the big picture, the picture of our love for our father.

Decades later, as young adults, both Sharon and I would find ourselves exploring the world.

Between us, we visited over eighty countries and hundreds of ports of call. I would eventually end up on Nantucket Island, and Sharon found her life two thousand miles away in Denver, Colorado.

One year we found it convenient to celebrate our thirtieth birthday together. We decided it would be grand to travel to our childhood home on Lake Drive and celebrate with Mom and Dad. They greeted us on the front porch with hugs and kisses.

Always, when returning home, it was amazing to see just how small our house really was and even more amazing to realize that at one time there had been eight of us living in this two-bedroom house—a small house with such big memories and such a big heart. When we entered the small living room, we could see on our right the even smaller dining room and the table that filled every square inch of the room. But it was what was on the table that caught our eyes. It was a pond boat . . . a sloop with a white and turquoise hull.

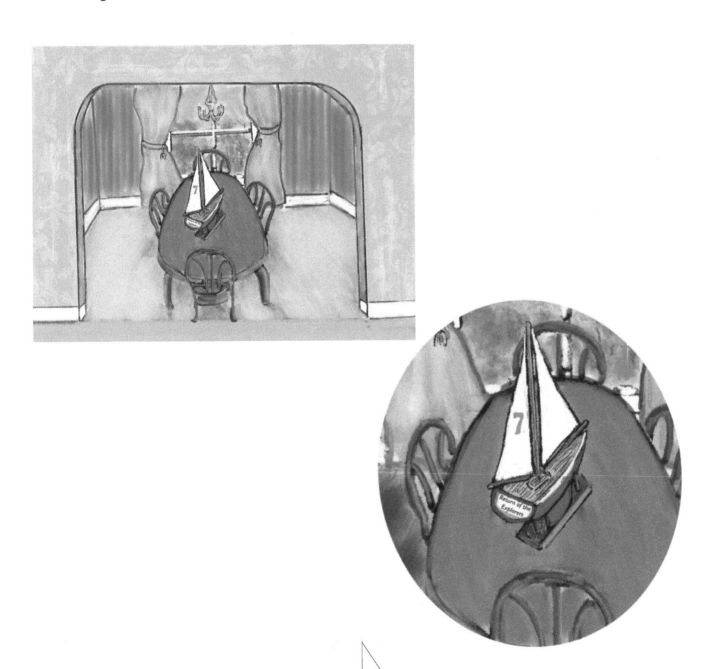

Dad had painted Sharon's name on the port side and my name on the starboard side. The three-foot sail had a number seven, hand sewn by my mother. On the stern below the transom Dad had painted in gold . . . *Return of the Explorers.*

We travel not to escape life, but for life not to escape us. –Unknown

Postscript

As I close my eyes, I can see clearly the memories of my childhood come into focus. Looking back, my father was an adventurous architect of an amazing personal life that was built upon a keen sense of creativity, curiosity, and the love of exploring the world outside the borders of our small backyard.

One of many memories that stands out, that combined all these marvelous character traits, was the day when our father presented a magnificent pond boat to us on our seventh birthday. I can see this as clear as day.

On that sun-filled day our father carried our boat, the *Explorer*, with us, his young captains, at his side to a small pond at the end of our street. It was here we would launch the *Explorer* on its maiden voyage. I can still feel the thrill. Putting the boat in the pond with pollywogs, turtles under lily pads that we knew all so well. Launching the pond boat, the *Explorer*, symbolized the beginning of a journey that Mark and I would take. We didn't know it at the time, but our future lives of world travel were being launched as well. Our father encouraged all his children to travel beyond the small pond of our youth and to the wider world and all the wonders it held.

My father would quote Alfred Lord Tennyson: "I am part of all that I have met." Our father instilled in us the desire to be curious, take risks, dream and discover new horizons. Anything is possible. There are no limits to what you can conquer.

My father traveled around the world. He appreciated all that crossed his path. He engaged all people and would share his travels with us when he returned home. Once inside the door he would open up his tattered brown suitcase that was full of stickers of places he had visited around the world. He had a gift for each of us, accompanied by fantastic stories of the amazing people he met along the way. We hung on every word and our desire to follow his path would become reality. Mark and I caught the wind in our sails and traveled to many harbors. Dreams do come true.

As I close my eyes and reflect on our return home years later, it exemplified the love of the pond boat, the *Explorer*, that began our journey. It would symbolize a journey to faraway lands and joyously coming home to a safe and loving harbor that my father and family provided.

By Sharon Duffield

Author

Mark Duffield has used his many and varied life experiences to write about the lessons learned in his youth that have provided a roadmap for those who navigate the uncertainties of daily living and inspire them to make sense of it. *AS I RECALL: The Explorer* draws upon Mark's past and his father's wisdom that laid the foundation for his travels abroad, a life at sea and the determination to write about how his life, and maybe yours, needs an inspired beginning. Other books by Mark Duffield include: *THE LAST SHEPARD and TALES OF THE TENTH ORNAMENT, AS I RECALL; Fireflies in the Night,* and *AS I RECALL; Wings of Remembrance.* Mark is currently a Media Consultant for Upstairs Downstairs on Beacon Hill in Boston.

Illustrator

Nancy O'Hearn is an accomplished artist/illustrator whose amazing and unique style has delighted all who follow the *AS I RECALL* series of stories. Self-taught and always experimenting, Nancy, after years as a local letter carrier, enjoys her current life of creating art and creating a working and loving life and environment for the dogs she cares for.

Other Works by Mark Duffield

The Last Shepard and Tales of the Tenth Ornament: A Wee Yarn of Wonder at Christmastime

AS I RECALL: Wings of Remembrance

AS I RECALL: Fireflies in the Night

COMING SOON

AS I RECALL: Mom's May Basket

Cover artwork by Sharon Duffield

Review Requested:

We'd like to know if you enjoyed the book.
Please consider leaving a review on the platform
from which you purchased the book.

CPSIA information can be obtained
at www.ICGtesting.com
Printed in the USA
BVHW022134310523
665188BV00001B/1